Wire and Findings

The array of findings on the market can be confusing to the novice, but relax. You only need a few items to begin.

You don't have to spend a lot of money to make something beautiful.

Beading supplies fall into three categories: stringing materials, beads, and findings. Stringing materials include beading or stringing wire, thread, and a variety of cords. Beads are the items being strung and are made of everything from stone to plastic. "Findings" is a jewelry term used to describe the parts that hold the piece together. Findings include clasps, ear wires, jump rings, split rings, crimp beads, crimp bead covers, wire guardians, head pins, and eye pins, just to name a few.

The best known string for simple strands is called beading wire.

Beadalon and Soft Flex are popular brands. Beading wire is made of stainless steel cables wrapped with a flexible nylon coating that makes the entire strand soft, bendable, and strong.

The spool label describes the number of strands, the diameter, the length, and sometimes the breaking tolerance, for example, 15 lbs.

For the projects in this book, we used 7 strand beading wire and Silver plated 19 strand wire.

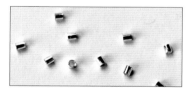

Crimp beads come in two shapes, tube and round. Crimp tubes are usually Sterling or Gold filled and the round ones are base metal.

Spacer beads are usually small to medium in size and are usually metallic. They make beautiful accents and add shine to any piece of jewelry.

Seed beads and E-beads in an array of colors including metallics make wonderful additions to use for spacing and fillers.

You will need a head pin for each dangle in your design.

Jump rings and split rings are used to connect clasps and special parts. Use a ring made from sturdy metal so it will hold its shape and be secure.

Clasps

A Toggle Clasp consists of a bar and a loop, circle, or other shape. Attach the bar to one end of the strand and the loop to the other end. To fasten, feed the bar through the loop.

A Lobster Claw clasp is both popular and secure. It can be used with a jump ring or a split ring.

An S hook clasp is interesting because it does ... rmanently ... n to the ... y piece. ... f the ... ten the ... ch part

Attaching a Clasp
for Bracelets and Necklaces

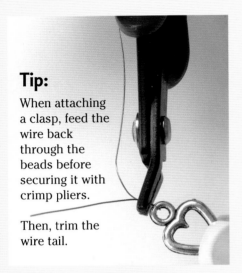

Tip:

When attaching a clasp, feed the wire back through the beads before securing it with crimp pliers.

Then, trim the wire tail.

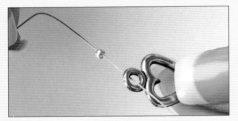

1. Thread a crimp bead and toggle clasp onto wire.

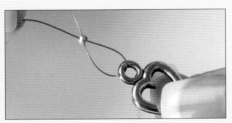

2. Thread the wire back through the crimp bead.

3. Crimp the bead.

String beads, pushing them down to cover the wire tails.

When you reach the other end, thread a crimp tube and the other section of the clasp. Pass the wire through the crimp tube and back through some beads. Crimp. Trim wire as needed.

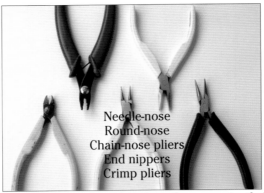

Needle-nose
Round-nose
Chain-nose pliers
End nippers
Crimp pliers

Basic Tools

There is a difference between jewelry pliers and those you find in the tool box in the garage. Open up the jaws of your pliers and look at the parts that hold your jewelry. You will see little lines or teeth. Using a handyman tool will mar the surface of your findings.

When just starting out, purchase the best tools you can afford. It's more cost effective to buy a good tool once than to buy inexpensive tools and replace them constantly because they don't work or they break. Good quality tools are easier to work with and will ensure a pleasant beading experience.

Beginning beaders need 5 basic tools. Chain-nose pliers have flat jaws that taper to a point. They are used to grip as well as bend wire. Round-nose pliers are essential for turning loops in head pins, eye pins and wire. Flat-nose pliers open and close jump rings. Crimp pliers are essential for closing crimp beads and tubes which keep your beads from falling off the ends of your wire. Finally, you need a good pair of wire cutters. Wire cutters come in two styles - end nippers and side cutters. Purchase both if your budget allows, but one or the other will get you started.

How to Close a Jump Ring

Grasp the ring on each side of the opening with pliers. Twist the ring sideways rather than pulling it open.

Making Earrings

Ear wires

Chandeliers

Earring findings are available in several shapes and sizes. Chandelier findings are metallic filigree with several tiny holes or loops for connecting additional pieces. They can be used as earrings or as end findings on necklaces with multiple strands.

Matching earrings complete a jewelry ensemble. The goal is to coordinate the pieces by repeating some elements in the necklace.

A simple way to make earrings is to use a head pin. Head pins are long wires with a head on one end. The diameter of the wire will vary so compare the diameter of the bead hole with the head pin.

Insert the pin through a sequence of beads. The remaining wire is bent into a round wrapped loop. Attach the loop to the ear wire and trim the wire tail.

1. Thread beads onto a head pin. Turn a loop at the top.

2. Finish a dangle with a wrapped loop.

3. Trim wire tail.

Glass Leaf Pendant Necklace

Imagine yourself strolling in the park on a sunny day - sunlight dappling the leaves - a light breeze fluffing your hair.

Capture that fresh air feeling in a necklace resplendent with the colors of nature.

MATERIALS:
- 1 glass Peridot Leaf 38x65mm
- 32 Olivine 4x6mm faceted rondelles
- 33 Amber 4mm faceted round beads
- 51 Clear size 6 E-beads
- 12 Clear 2mm beads
- 1 Silver toggle clasp
- 2 Silver crimp tubes
- 22" of 7 strand beading wire

INSTRUCTIONS: SIZE - 17":

String 1 Amber bead onto the center of the wire.

Center the pendant over the bead.

On each side of the pendant, string the following pattern: Olivine-E-Amber-E.

Repeat the pattern 12 times.

Repeat the pattern 3 more times using 2mm Clear beads in place of the E-beads.

Attach each section of the clasp with a crimp tube.

Gemstone Necklace

Like birthstones and months of the year, each gemstone is connected to a sign of the Zodiac. Fall in love with the patterns of Pink Feldspar, Green Epidote and Quartz found in Chinese Unakite. This stone is believed to have cleansing, balancing and detoxifying properties while the quartz adds an affiliation with affairs of the heart.

MATERIALS:
- 3 Chinese Unakite 30mm donut beads
- 6 Chinese Unakite 4mm round beads
- 3 Silver 24 gauge wires 2" long
- 1 Silver 18" chain

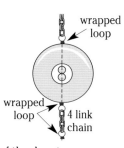

INSTRUCTIONS: SIZE - 19":

Cut the chain in half.

Cut a 4-link piece from each cut end.

Attach a wire to each cut end of the chain with a wrapped loop.

Pass each wire through 1 side of a donut bead.

Add 2 round beads and pass the wire through the other side of the donut.

Form a wrapped loop attaching an end of a 4-link chain.

Attach 1 end of a 4 link chain to the remaining wire with a wrapped loop.

Pass the wire into the center donut and thread 2 beads as before.

Connect the remaining 4-link chain with a wrapped loop.

Turquoise Teardrop Necklace

Dripping with silky texture and the weight of genuine stone, this necklace will take you back to the days when only royalty wore such luxury.

Indulge your senses with this fabulous accessory today.

MATERIALS:
- 30 *Swarovski* Aquamarine 4mm crystals
- 14 Turquoise dyed Howlite 13x18mm drops
- 36 Turquoise dyed Howlite 4mm round beads
- 15 Silver 4mm cube beads
- 1 Silver toggle clasp
- 2 Crimp tubes
- 20" of 7-strand beading wire

INSTRUCTIONS: SIZE - 16":

String a Silver bead onto the center of the wire.
On each side, string a 4mm Turquoise and a crystal.
On each end of the wire string the following pattern:
  Drop-crystal-4mm Turquoise-Silver-4mm Turquoise-crystal.
Repeat this pattern 5 times.
End with a drop-crystal-4mm Turquoise-Silver-crystal-
  4 Turquoise 4mm round beads.
Attach a section of the clasp to each end with a crimp tube.

Pearl Loop Necklace

Fast and fabulous! Create a sumptuous group of pearl and turquoise dangles with a simple stringing technique. This light and wispy necklace is sure to become an everyday favorite. Novice beaders will find it easy to accomplish a quality designer look.

MATERIALS:
- 136 glass pearls 4mm
- 3 Turquoise dyed Howlite 13x18mm drops
- 7 Silver 3mm cubes
- 1 Silver toggle clasp
- 2 Crimp tubes
- 25" of 7-strand beading wire

INSTRUCTIONS: SIZE - 16":

Attach one end of the clasp to the
  wire with a crimp tube.
String: 1 pearl-1 cube-20 pearls-
  1 cube-20 pearls-1 cube-
  7 pearls-1 teardrop-7 pearls.
Pass the wire through the cube
  forming a loop.
Pull gently to make the beads snug.
String: 6 pearls-1 cube-7 pearls-
  1 teardrop-7 pearls.
Pass the wire through the cube as before, forming the middle loop.
String 6 pearls-1 cube-7 pearls-1 teardrop-7 pearls.
Pass the wire through the cube to form the third loop.
String 20 pearls-1 cube-20 pearls-1 cube-1 pearl.
Attach the other section of the clasp with a crimp tube.

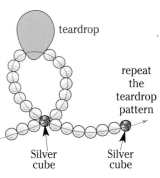

teardrop

repeat
the
teardrop
pattern

Silver
cube

Silver
cube

Turquoise Cross Necklace

Turquoise is one of the official birthstones for the month of December. This lustrous gem has been treasured by cultures all over the world for thousands of years.

Now you can create your own turquoise treasure with this alluring design.

MATERIALS:
- 1 Turquoise Cross pendant 28mm x 55mm including bail
- 6 Turquoise 13mm x 18mm oval beads
- 8 Silver 8mm tube beads
- 16 Silver 5mm round beads
- 3 Silver 2mm round beads
- 1 Silver toggle clasp
- 2 Crimp tubes
- 20" Silver plated 19-strand beading wire

INSTRUCTIONS: SIZE - 16½":
String 3 Silver 2mm beads.
Place them in the center of the wire.
Center the pendant over the 2mm beads.
On each end of the wire string the following pattern:
　　Round-Tube-Round-Turquoise oval.
Repeat pattern for 3 Turquoise beads on each side of the pendant.
End each wire with a Round-Tube-Round.
Attach a section of the clasp to each end with a crimp tube.

Pearl & Turquoise Ensemble

Resplendent with reflective light, these pearls are destined to enhance the beauty of someone special. Bright, lustrous and lightweight, this genuine stone ensemble is a joy to wear.

MATERIALS:
- 10 Natural Pearl 12mm lentil beads (2 for earrings)
- 31 Natural Stone Turquoise beads (8 for earrings)
- 2 Pearl 4mm round beads (for earrings)
- 6 Aqua 2mm beads
- 1 Silver toggle clasp • 2 Crimp tubes
- 2 Silver ear wires and 2 Silver 3" head pins (for earrings)
- 10" of 7-strand beading wire

BRACELET INSTRUCTIONS: SIZE - 7½" :
String 3 Turquoise beads onto the center of the wire.
On each side, string the following pattern: Pearl- 3 Turquoise.
Repeat the pattern twice.
End with a Pearl-Turquoise-3 Aqua beads.
Attach a section of the clasp to each end with a crimp tube.

EARRING INSTRUCTIONS:
String the following on a head pin:
　　round Pearl-Turquoise-lentil Pearl- 3 Turquoise-round pearl.
Attach to the ear wire with a turned loop. Make 2.

Turquoise & Coral Ensemble

Make a bold fashion statement and get dressed with attitude. Coral and turquoise energetically combine in this flashy ensemble.

MATERIALS:
- 11 Red Coral 18x12mm beads (4 for bracelet, 2 for earrings)
- 32 Red Coral round 4mm beads (10 for bracelet, 2 for earrings)
- 20 Turquoise 12mm disk beads (6 for bracelet, 2 for earrings)
- 20 Silver 2x5mm spacer beads (6 for bracelet, 2 for earrings)
- 2 Silver toggle clasps (1 for bracelet)
- 4 Crimp tubes (2 for bracelet) • 4 Crimp bead covers (2 for bracelet)
- 7-strand beading wire (20" for necklace, 12" for bracelet)
- 2 Silver 3" head pins and 2 Silver ear wires (for earrings)

NECKLACE INSTRUCTIONS: SIZE - 13":
Thread a large Red bead onto the center of the wire.
On each side of the wire, string the following:
  spacer-small Red-2 disks-small Red-spacer-large Red.
Repeat the pattern once.
String: spacer-small Red-2 disks-4 small Red-spacer-small Red.
Attach a clasp to each end of the wire with a crimp tube.
Squeeze a crimp bead cover over the crimp tube.

BRACELET INSTRUCTIONS - SIZE: 7½:" :
Attach the bar section of the clasp to 1 end of the wire with a crimp tube • Squeeze a crimp bead cover over the crimp tube.
• Thread 3 small Red beads. • String the following:
  large Red-spacer-small Red-2 disks-small Red-spacer.
Repeat the pattern twice. • Thread a large Red and 1 small Red bead. • Attach the other section of the clasp with a crimp tube.
• Squeeze a crimp bead cover over the crimp tube.

EARRING INSTRUCTIONS:
Thread a large Red-spacer-disk-small Red bead onto a head pin.
Attach to ear wire with a wrapped loop. Make 2.

Turquoise & Coral Necklace

Corallium rubrum is a species of marine coral known as precious coral or red coral. Coveted for the intensity of its color, fine jewelers have incorporated coral in masterpieces for centuries. Now you can wear one of nature's most durable gifts in a necklace.

MATERIALS:
- 3 Red Coral 18x12mm beads - 16 Red Coral round 4mm beads
- 2 *Swarovski* Lt. Siam 8mm round crystals
- 8 Turquoise 19mm disk beads • 8 Turquoise 15mm disk beads
- 14 Turquoise 4mm round beads • 6 Silver 5mm modern rondelle beads
- 4 Silver 5mm daisy single spacer beads • 1 Silver toggle clasp
- 2 Crimp tubes • 3 Silver 3" head pins • 22" piece of 7-strand beading wire

INSTRUCTIONS: SIZE - 18":
Dangles: On each head pin, thread the following: 4mm Turquoise-large Coral-4mm Turquoise. • Form a wrapped loop at the top.
Necklace: Center a dangle on the wire. • On each side of the dangle, string the following rondelle-Coral round-rondelle-dangle-rondelle. • String a Coral round-19mm Turquoise disk. Repeat the pattern 3 times. • String a daisy spacer-crystal-daisy spacer. • String a 15mm disk-4mm Coral. • Repeat the pattern twice. • End with a 15mm disk and 4 Turquoise 4mm round beads.
Clasp: Attach the clasp with a crimp tube.

Glass Pendant Necklace

Absolutely awesome! The iridescent swirl in this pendant will have all your friends zooming in for a closer look. This designer piece derives its style from the beads chosen to coordinate with the swirling colors in the pendant.

MATERIALS:
- 1 *Blue Moon* Glass pendant 42x55mm
- 16 *Blue Moon* Dark Red stone 10mm round beads
- 44 Aqua 3x6mm faceted rondelles
- 2 Clear 4mm beads
- 20 Silver 5mm daisy double spacer beads
- 18 Silver 5mm daisy single spacer beads
- 1 Silver toggle clasp
- 2 Crimp tubes
- 22" of 7-strand beading wire

INSTRUCTIONS: SIZE - $16\frac{1}{2}$":
String 2 Clear 4mm beads. Place them in the center of the wire.
Center the pendant over the 4mm beads.
On each side of the pendant, string the following pattern:
Red-double spacer-2 Aqua-double spacer.
Repeat the pattern 4 times.
Repeat the pattern 3 more times using single spacers in place of the double spacers.
String: 2 Aqua-single spacer.
Repeat 2 times.
Attach a section of the clasp to each end with a crimp tube.

Turquoise Donut Bracelet

Whimsical and dynamic, the donuts give this bracelet a fun shape. Interwoven strands are a lighthearted departure from the same old straight line stringing.

Make a matching necklace by increasing the number of donuts to four or six for an ensemble that you will love.

MATERIALS:
- 2 Turquoise dyed Howlite 35mm donuts
- 5 Turquoise dyed Howlite 15x10mm tube beads
- 46 Red dyed Coral 5mm round beads
- 1 Silver toggle clasp
- 2 Crimp tubes • 2 Silver crimp tube covers
- 2 pieces of 7-strand beading wire 12" long

INSTRUCTIONS: SIZE - 8":
Attach both wires to one section of the clasp with a crimp tube.
Pass both wires through 2 Red-1 tube-1 Red-1 tube.
Separate the wires.
String 10 Red beads on each wire.
Weave each wire through the donut as shown in the diagram.
Pass both wires through a Turquoise tube.
Separate the wires again and repeat the Red beads and donut.
Pass both wires through a tube-Red bead-tube-2 Red beads.
Attach both wires to the other part of the clasp with a crimp tube.
Press a crimp bead cover over each crimp tube.

crimp

Blue Heart
Necklace & Earrings

Complement the cooler colors of your wardrobe with an alluring combination of smoke, blue and jet.

A stunning heart takes center stage with a glittering supporting cast of crystals for an ensemble with uptown appeal and distinctive style.

MATERIALS:
  1 Sapphire heart pendant 33x30x16mm
  36 Opaque Blue 6x8mm faceted rondelles (8 for earrings)
  20 Jet 6mm bicone crystals (4 for earrings)
  44 Jet 4mm bicone crystals (6 for earrings)
  57 Smoke 4mm bicone crystals (30 for earrings)
  2 Clear size 6 E-beads
  1 Silver toggle clasp • 2 Crimp tubes
  12 Silver 2" head pins (for earrings)
  2 Silver chandelier ear wires (for earrings)
  22" of 7-strand beading wire

NECKLACE INSTRUCTIONS: SIZE - 19":
String 2 Clear E-beads.
Place them in the center of the wire.
Center the pendant over the E-beads.
On each side of the pendant, string the following pattern:
  Blue-6mm Jet-Smoke-6mm Jet
  Repeat the pattern 3 times.
Repeat the pattern 9 more times using 4mm Jet bicones
  in place of the 6mm Jet bicones.
Clasp: On 1 end, add 1 Blue bead.
Attach the bar section of the clasp with a crimp tube.
On the other end, string a Blue-4mm Jet-4mm Smoke-4mm Jet.
Attach the circle section of the clasp with a crimp tube.
EARRING INSTRUCTIONS:
Top dangle: On a head pin, thread Smoke-Blue-Smoke crystals.
Bottom dangles #1, #3 & #5: On a head pin, thread the following crystals: Smoke-Blue-Smoke-4mm Jet-Smoke.
Bottom dangles #2 & #4: On a head pin, thread the following crystals: Smoke-6mm Jet-Smoke.
Attach each dangle to the chandelier with a wrapped loop.

Turquoise
and Pearl
Bracelets

Polished to a touchable smoothness, natural stone beads attract your hand as well as your eye.

The luster of pearls combined with the beauty of turquoise create the perfect balance in these beautiful bracelets.

TURQUOISE AND PEARLS BRACELET MATERIALS:
  3 Turquoise 25x35mm oval beads
  12 Freshwater Pearl 4x6mm rice beads
  1 Silver toggle clasp • 2 Crimp tubes
  12" of 7-strand beading wire

TURQUOISE AND PEARLS BRACELET INSTRUCTIONS: SIZE - 7½":
Attach the bar section of the clasp to the wire with a crimp tube.
String 3 sets of 3 pearls-1 Turquoise. String 3 pearls.
Attach the ring section of the clasp with a crimp tube.

FRESHWATER PEARLS BRACELET MATERIALS:
  20 Freshwater Pearl 8x9mm potato beads
  9 Turquoise dyed Howlite 4mm beads
  1 Silver toggle clasp • 2 Crimp tubes
  12" of 7-strand beading wire

FRESHWATER PEARLS BRACELET INSTRUCTIONS: SIZE - 7½":
Attach the bar section of the clasp to the wire with a crimp tube.
String 2 Turquoise beads.
String 6 sets of 3 pearls-1 Turquoise.
String 2 pearls and 1 Turquoise. Attach the ring section of the clasp with a crimp tube.

Blue Spiral Pendant Necklace

Man has always been fascinated by the spiral. For millenia, this intriguing natural shape has been a favorite artistic motif.

A fabulous glass spiral forms the focal point of a superb necklace.

MATERIALS:
- 1 Amethyst Lampwork curl pendant 50x33x15mm
- 22 Aqua 3x6mm faceted rondelles
- 22 Amber 6mm diamond cut crystals
- 6 Aqua 4mm bicone crystals
- 49 Silver 4mm spacer beads
- 5 Clear size 6 E-beads
- 1 Silver toggle clasp • 3 Crimp tubes
- 25" and 4" of 7-strand beading wire

INSTRUCTIONS: SIZE - 17":

4" Wire for the Pendant:
String 6 pairs of 4mm beads:
    Silver ball-Aqua bicone.
Pass string through the pendant.
Add an E-bead and crimp tube.
Pull the wire ends to form a
    snug circle. Crimp.
Position the crimp tube so it will be
    covered by the pendant.

pull wire snug, make equal lengths

25" wire

crimp

25" Wire for the Necklace:
Feed the wire through the circle, bringing each end
    through a spacer bead from opposite directions.
On each side of the spacer bead, string the following:
    Aqua-spacer-Amber-spacer.
Repeat the pattern 9 times.
Finish with an Aqua-spacer-Amber-2 E-beads.
Attach a section of the clasp to each wire with a crimp tube.

*Beading is a
wonderful pastime...
You don't have to spend
a lot of money to make
something beautiful.*

Natural Stone Ensemble

Organic Black Lava stones possess a very natural, earthy appeal. This bracelet is full of fabulous texture, combining the pumice of volcanic stone, the veins of howlite, and the carved design of silver for a statement that is strong, vibrant and fresh.

MATERIALS:
- 8 Turquoise dyed Howlite 15x10mm tube beads (2 for earrings)
- 5 Jet 20mm stone beads (2 for earrings)
- 14 Silver 4mm round beads (2 for earrings)
- 1 Silver toggle clasp • 2 Silver 12mm bead caps
- 2 Silver crimp tubes • 2 Silver crimp bead covers
- 15" of 7-strand beading wire
- 2 Silver ear wires (for earrings)
- 2 Silver 12mm bead caps (for earrings)
- 2 Silver 4" head pins (for earrings)

BRACELET INSTRUCTIONS: SIZE - 9":
String a Black bead onto the center of the wire.
On each end of the wire string the following pattern:
    Silver-Turquoise-Silver-Black-Silver-Turquoise-Silver-Turquoise.
Thread each end of the wire into a bead cap and 2 Silver beads.
Attach a section of the clasp to each end with a crimp tube.
Press a crimp bead cover over each crimp bead.

EARRING INSTRUCTIONS:
String a Black-Silver-Turquoise-bead cap onto a head pin.
Attach to the ear wire with a turned loop. Make 2.

Turquoise & Silver Ensemble

An irresistible combination, silver and turquoise are a traditional pairing that guarantees a sensational look every time. Perfect when you need a quick gift for someone special, you can make this set in about an hour.

MATERIALS:
- 10 Turquoise dyed Howlite 12mm flat beads (4 for earrings)
- 7 Silver 15mm handmade disks (2 for earrings)
- 3 Silver 4mm round beads
- 1 Silver toggle clasp • 2 Silver crimp tubes
- 10" of 7-strand beading wire
- 2 Silver ear wires (for earrings)
- 2 Silver 4" head pins (for earrings)

BRACELET INSTRUCTIONS: SIZE - 7":
Attach one end of the wire to the bar end of the clasp with a crimp tube.
String 2 Silver round beads.
String a Turquoise-Silver disk. Repeat the pattern 4 times.
End with a Turquoise and Silver round bead.
Attach the other end of the clasp with a crimp tube.

EARRING INSTRUCTIONS:
String a Turquoise-Silver disk-Turquoise onto a head pin.
Attach to the ear wire with a turned loop. Make 2.

Turquoise & Crystal Ensemble

Archaeologists have discovered turquoise jewelry dating back to 900 b.c. This fabulous stone has a long tradition of enhancing the beauty of nobility and royalty. Now you can join their ranks with this exquisite designer ensemble of lustrous stone and twinkling crystals.

MATERIALS:

16 Turquoise 20mm disks - 22 Turquoise 12mm disks
22 Turquoise 10x15mm tube beads (2 for earrings)
17 Clear 8mm crystals • 21 Clear 6mm crystals (2 for earrings)
23 Clear 4mm crystals (2 for earrings)
176 Seafoam size 11 seed beads • 1 Silver 22mm 3-hole bar clasp
6 Silver crimp tubes
7-strand beading wire (18", 20", 24")
2 Silver ear wires (for earrings) • 2 Silver 3" head pins (for earrings)

NECKLACE INSTRUCTIONS: SIZE - 16":

Top Wire: Attach the 18" wire to the top hole in the bar with a crimp tube. • String 5 seed beads-a 12mm disk-seed-4mm crystal-seed. • Repeat the pattern 18 times. • End with a 12mm disk and 5 seed beads. • Attach wire to the top hole in the second bar with a crimp tube.

Middle Wire: Attach the 20" wire to the center hole in the bar with a crimp tube. • String 7 seed beads. • String a Turquoise tube-seed-6mm crystal-seed. • Repeat the pattern 18 times. • End with a Turquoise tube and 7 seed beads. • Attach the wire to the center hole in the second bar with a crimp tube.

Bottom Wire: Attach the 24" wire to the bottom hole in the bar with a crimp tube. • String 20 seed beads. • String an 8mm crystal-seed-20mm disk-seed. • Repeat the pattern 15 times. • End with an 8mm crystal and 20 seed beads. • Attach wire with a crimp tube.

EARRING INSTRUCTIONS:

String a 6mm crystal-Turquoise tube-4mm crystal onto a head pin. Attach to the ear wire with a turned loop. Make 2.

crimp

Turquoise and Crystal Bracelet

Combining crystal with stone creates an appealing result every time. Varying the size of stones and crystals adds interest while the sparkle invites one's eye for a closer inspection. Experiment with your bead and crystal collection to create new and exciting looks.

MATERIALS:

5 Turquoise 14mm round faceted beads • 6 Clear AB 8mm round crystals
18 *Swarovski* Aquamarine 4mm crystals
2 Crimp bead covers • 1 Silver toggle clasp • 2 Crimp tubes
15" Silver plated 19-strand beading wire

INSTRUCTIONS: SIZE - 7½":

Center a Turquoise bead on the wire. • On each end of the wire, string the following pattern: Aquamarine-Clear-Aquamarine-Turquoise. Repeat the pattern once.
String: Aquamarine-Clear-4 Aquamarine crystals on each end. • Attach a section of the clasp to each end with a crimp tube. • Squeeze a crimp bead cover over each crimp bead.

Black and Gold Ensemble

Whether you appreciate the clean lines or the exotic goth character, this exciting choker and earring set has undeniable appeal. Make it this afternoon - dazzle your friends this evening.

MATERIALS:
- 19 Jet glass 10x25mm sharp oval beads (2 for earrings)
- 8 Clear 4mm crystals (for earrings)
- 20 Gold plated spiral 6mm beads (4 for earrings)
- 66 Clear 2mm E-beads (16 for earrings)
- 1 Gold toggle clasp • 4 Crimp tubes (2 for earrings)
- 16 Clear 2mm E-beads • 2 Silver ear wires (for earrings)
- 7-strand beading wire (16" and two 5" for earrings)

NECKLACE INSTRUCTIONS: SIZE - 14":
Attach the wire to 1 section of the clasp with a crimp tube.
String 9 E-beads. String a Jet oval- E-Gold-E.
Repeat the pattern 15 times. End with a Jet oval and 9 E-beads.
Attach the other section of the clasp with a crimp tube.

EARRING INSTRUCTIONS:
Center a Jet oval on a wire.
On each side, string
    a crystal-Gold bead-
    crystal-4 E-beads.
Thread on the ear wire and a
    crimp tube.
Pass each end of wire through
    the crimp tube from
    different directions.
Pull gently to form a circle.
Crimp together. Make 2.

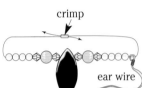

Trio of Bracelets

So many choices, so little time! Whether you wear these bracelets together on the same arm or separately, you will love the burnished glow of the gold and the twinkle of jet and crystal.

This winning combination with its class, flash and brass, says "notice me!"

MATERIALS:
- 25 Jet 9x12mm faceted rondelles
- 14 Gold melon corrugated 8x12mm beads
- 12 Gold plated diamond cut spiral 6mm beads
- 49 Clear 2mm E-beads • 6 Clear size 11 seed beads • 3 Clear 8mm crystals
- 3 Gold toggle clasps - 6 Crimp tubes
- 7-strand beading wire (3 pieces 10" long)

INSTRUCTIONS FOR EACH BRACELET: SIZE - 7 TO 8" each:
Attach the wire to a bar section of the clasp with a crimp tube.
String the beads by referring to the photo for placement and size.
TIP: Develop a pattern of beads then repeat it to the end of each bracelet.
Attach the other section of the clasp with a crimp tube.

Red Glass Ensemble

Bold and flashy, this jewelry blazes with red-hot energy. The swirl and shape of the glass beads give this ensemble a clever, art-deco appeal that demands attention.

MATERIALS:
- 5 Red Venitian glass 12x20mm bicone beads (2 for earrings)
- 3 Red glass 12mm round beads
- 18 Black 6mm bicone crystals (4 for earrings)
- 9 Clear 6mm round beads (2 for earrings)
- 1 Silver toggle clasp
- 2 Silver crimp tubes
- 12" of 7-strand beading wire
- 2 Silver ear wires (for earrings)
- 2 Silver 4" head pins (for earrings)

BRACELET INSTRUCTIONS: SIZE - 8":
Attach one end of the wire to the bar end of the clasp with a crimp tube.
String Black-Clear-Black-12mm Red-Black-Clear-Black-Red bicone. Repeat the pattern 2 times. End with a Black-Clear-Black.
Attach the other end of the clasp with a crimp tube.

EARRING INSTRUCTIONS:
String a Black-Red-Clear-Black onto a head pin.
Attach to the ear wire with a turned loop. Make 2.

Just in Time Watch

Add instant pizzazz to your wardrobe and turn your watch into a timeless treasure suitable for every occasion, twenty-four hours a day.

Natural coral chips give this timepiece a personality as unique as your own.

MATERIALS:
- 1 Watch face
- 50 Red Coral chips
- 2 Turquoise dyed Howlite 15x10mm tube beads
- 2 Turquoise 12mm disk beads
- 4 Clear 6x6mm crystal cubes
- 16 Silver 4mm round beads
- 12 Silver crimp tubes
- 6 pieces of 7-strand beading wire 5" long
- 4 Silver 3-hole slider bars 13mm long
- 2 Silver 3-hole bars 21mm long with clasp
- 2 clamps or tape to secure wires.

INSTRUCTIONS: WATCH SIZE - 7":
Attach a wire to each hole in one section of the clasp bar with a crimp tube. • String a Silver ball on each wire. • Pass all 3 wires through the holes in a slider bar. • String the following on the center wire: Crystal-Silver ball-disk-Silver ball-Crystal. • Clamp the center wire to keep the beads snug. • On each outer wire, string Coral chips to fill the space. Coral chips are not uniform in size, so each side may have a different number of chips. • Pass all 3 wires through the holes of the second slider bar. • Clamp the 2 outer wires. • String a Turquoise tube on the middle wire. • Clamp the wire to secure. • On each outer wire, string Coral chips to fill the space. • String a Silver ball on each wire. • Attach each wire to the watch with a crimp tube. • Repeat these instructions for the other side of the watch.

Purple Pendant Necklace

Got bling? This sassy necklace with gleaming crystals provides a perfect complement for a flashy dichroic glass pendant. You'll want to wear this easy-to-assemble beauty every day, and your friends will want one too!

MATERIALS:
    1 Pink/Black dichroic glass pendant 25x25mm
    8 Pink dichroic glass 4x6mm beads
    16 Clear 4x6mm crystal rondelles
    2 Purple 6mm bicone crystals
    40 Black 4mm bicone beads
    32 Clear 2mm beads
    1 Silver toggle clasp • 4 Silver crimp tubes
    20" of Silver plated 19-strand beading wire

INSTRUCTIONS: SIZE - 18":
Center the pendant on the wire.
String a Purple crystal on each side of the pendant.
On each side of the pendant, string the following pattern:
    Jet-rondelle-Jet-rondelle-Jet-Pink glass.
Repeat the pattern 3 times.
String the following pattern: Jet-2 Clear 2mm beads.
Repeat the pattern 7 times. End with a crimp tube.
Make sure the beads are centered on the wire. Crimp.
Attach each section of the clasp with a crimp tube.

Silver Charm Bracelet

Whether you wear a charm bracelet because you love the jingle, the variety of shapes, or the feeling of movement on your wrist, this is an accessory you will enjoy every day.

MATERIALS:
    1 *Swarovski* Silver 7" chain • 9 Silver assorted charms
    9 Silver 8mm split rings • 2 Silver jump rings
    1 Silver toggle clasp
INSTRUCTIONS: SIZE - 7":
Attach charms to bracelet with split rings.
Attach clasp to bracelet with jump rings.

Travel Charm Bracelet

Whether you travel the world or only dream of doing so, discover the joys of collecting charms that symbolize your adventures with this fun bracelet.

MATERIALS:
    1 Silver 8" chain with clasp
    5 *Blue Moon* Silver travel charms
    Assorted leftover beads and crystals
    12 head pins • 15" Silver 24 gauge wire
INSTRUCTIONS: SIZE - 8" including clasp:
Make 12 dangles by threading assorted beads and
    crystals on head pins.
Attach each dangle with a wrapped loop.
Use wire to attach each charm with a wrapped loop.

Silver Starfish Necklace

Simple, discerning, classy, and smart... silver accessories complement every color in your wardrobe. This fabulous necklace will brighten and add a touch of glitz to your day.

Silver Starfish Necklace

MATERIALS:

- 1 Silver starfish pendant 60x60mm
- 12 Silver 12x12mm chunk beads
- 48 Silver 5mm bicone beads
- 92 Clear 2mm beads • 2 Clear size 6 E-beads
- 2 Silver 14mm 3-hole bars
- 1 Silver toggle clasp • 2 Silver crimp bead covers
- Silver plated 19-strand beading wire (two 7", one 10", one 12")

INSTRUCTIONS: SIZE - 18":

10" wire: String 2 E-beads onto the center of the wire. • String the pendant over the E-beads. • On each side of the pendant, string: bicone-2 Clear beads. • Repeat this pattern 15 times. End with a Clear bead. • Attach the wire to the top hole of a 3-hole bar with a crimp tube, making the beads snug.

12" wire: Pass the wire through both E-beads and the pendant. • On each side of the pendant, string a bicone and 1 Clear bead. • String the following pattern: Chunk- Clear-bicone-Clear. • Repeat this pattern 5 times. • Attach the wire to the bottom hole of a 3-hole bar with a crimp tube making the beads snug.

Clasp: Following the diagram, attach each 7" wire to the 3-hole bar with a crimp tube. Press a crimp tube cover over each crimp tube. Attach the other end of each 7" wire to a section of the clasp with a crimp tube.

Green Glass Pendant Choker

Capture the mild touch of soft meadow grass in Springtime with this delicate necklace. Its subtle curves embrace your neck with whisper-soft beads and lighthearted fashion.

The quiet style of this gorgeous glass pendant will draw everyone in for a closer look.

MATERIALS:

    1 Glass pendant 38x38mm
    24 Opaque Green 6x8mm faceted rondelles
    16 Clear 4x6mm crystal rondelles
    500 Clear size 11 seed beads
    1 Silver crimp bead cover
    1 Silver toggle clasp
    4 Silver crimp tubes
    7-strand beading wire (two 4", three 25")
    2 clamps
    Tape or T-pin

INSTRUCTIONS: SIZE - 13":

Necklace:
Attach all three 25" wires to the circle portion
    of the clasp with a crimp tube. Crimp.
Secure the clasp to a work surface with tape or a T-pin.

Middle Wire:
Pass the wire through 5 seed beads and a Green
    rondelle.
Repeat until all rondelles are used.
End with 5 seed beads.
Clamp the wire to prevent the beads falling off.

Outer Wires:
String one wire completely. Clamp.
Then string the last wire.
Both wires are strung in the same manner as the
    middle wire, using 7 seed beads instead of 5.

Necklace Finish:
Gently pull the middle wire so the beads
    fit snugly; this will cause the outer wires to
    curve.
Attach all 3 wires to the other section of the clasp
    with a crimp tube. Crimp.

Pendant Loop:
Using a 4" wire, string the pendant,
    12 seed beads and a crimp tube.
Pass the wires through the crimp from
    opposite directions.
Gently pull the wire ends to form a
    loop. Crimp.

Pendant Bail:
Using another 4" wire, repeat this process,
    passing through the first loop rather than
    the pendant and through the center of
    the necklace.
Press a crimp bead cover over the crimp tube.

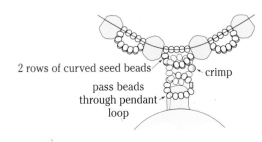

2 rows of curved seed beads   crimp

pass beads through pendant loop

*Debra Rohlfing is an accomplished beader who teaches beading at the **Artful Bead** store in Texas.*

A special thanks to Debra for expertly making all of the beautiful jewelry in this book.